DEEPENING GROOVE

DEEPENING GROOVE

Ravi Shankar

For the substance of things.

RV

NYC · 11/20 15

The National Poetry Review Press
Aptos, California

The National Poetry Review Press
(an imprint of DHP)
Post Office Box 2080, Aptos, California 95001-2080

Printed in the United States of America
Published in 2011 by The National Poetry Review Press

ISBN 978-1-935716-08-2

Artwork by Patricia Van Lubeck, vanlubeck.com
"Tilia ora"
120 x 80 cm oil painting

CONTENTS

Let us examine if it finite be.
—Lucretius

Crossings

Between forest & field, a threshold
like stepping from a cathedral into the street—
the quality of air alters, an eclipse lifts,

boundlessness opens, earth itself retextured
into weeds where woods once were.
Even planes of motion shift from vertical

navigation to horizontal quiescence:
there's a standing invitation to lie back
as sky's unpredictable theater proceeds.

Suspended in this ephemeral moment
after leaving a forest, before entering
a field, the nature of reality is revealed.

Buzzards

Gregarious in hunger, a flock of twenty
turn circles like whorls of barbed wire,
no spot below flown over uncanvassed.

The closer to death the closer they come,
waiting on wings with keen impatient
perseverance, dark blades lying in wake

until age or wound has turned canter
into carcass or near enough for them
to swoop scrupulous in benediction,

land hissing, hopping, tearing, gorging.
no portion, save bone, too durable
to digest. What matters cannot remain.

Oyster

Gnarled as cliff-face, two shells suctioned,
one snug in another to shape a rocky pear,
bluish, held together by a dark protein hinge,

content once in spatfall on a piling, changed
from free-swimming to inert life filtering
plankton from water, beating cilia. Dredged

firmaments of bread & brine now on ice
with lemon wedges in a fish stall window.
Soft, protandric pulsations in mantle skirts

made liquid to itself, turning males female
& back again, telling secrets that require
a knife to pry open & vinegar to serve.

for Sandra Beasley

Sand

From the meeting of sediment with epoch,
a spectrum materializes in ochre, in clay,
in bronzed loam, else friable, gray, broken

from the centuries in crumbled grade
not gravel, nor silt, closer to dredge
than detritus, carpets of peppercorn-sized

grains laid earthwise in wind, by stream,
bandied minuscule in sphericity to tend
feldspar banks, to feed foundries silica,

to constellate on dunes in undulating drift,
flakes polished by a slow crash of crusts
recurrent underfoot, ground down in time.

Palm Tree

Between the art deco Celebrity 5 & 10
& Ripley's Odditorium, dwarfing even
the Yamashiro Sky Room's glass enclosed

gaze, all that remains of mangrove wetlands
are not here: row upon row of cyclopean
sentries, fibrous, outsize & rough-hewn,

fronds a diadem for drupes too high to see.
Like the billboards, they're transplants
imported from the Canary Islands a century

ago by wildcatters who staked their claim
by force, putting down roots & drill bits
while husked trunks lengthened to the stars.

Primitives

Banish the glaze of objects from the firmament,
undo formica & fundament, pinch off the ridges
of the Caucasus & irons of clay used in hearths
some four millennia ago. Ask how blind urges
creolized in burnished arabesque surfaces
that once glowed in fire are now backlit in humidity-
controlled glass capsules indexed by number,
defined by placard, sold at auction. Recall
that clusters of bird bones found buried with relics
are those of Gallus gallus—the domestic chicken.
Trace a chain of Y-chromosomes from the Upper
Paleolithic imagination to rock walls scarred
with petroglyphs & handprints. To poems.
Burnish the gaze of subjects with firm remnants.

Tideline

Sand bar scored across the flooded marshes,
resolving upon closer inspection into patches—
chaffweed, arrow arum, sweet flag, halberd-

leaved tearthumb, cinquefoil well-withered
of inflorescence by the sun, stones polished
smooth by the wavelets' incessant mantra—

watch, catch, wash, cash, wished, clasp, plash—
polyrhythmic percussion lightening, darkening
over bright afternoon's fuzzed-out jazz sax,

sprats squirting through slippery brown mounds
of bladderwrack which might feel to our soles,
kept dry in shoes, like the very pulp of love.

for Gray Jacobik

Stingray

Encircled by vast panes of tank, fish in transit
a clock's second hand, schools ending
where they began to begin again, while below,

near pebbled substrate & transplanted sea
grass, a silhouetted parallelogram moves
sinuous, a hawk flapping, a space age vessel

all blunt stealth & cartilaginous grace, tail
a whip barbed with fingernail stingers, eyes
flattened away from a vacuum-cleaner mouth.

A ray, in mathematics, extends indefinitely
in both directions; here, fed blackworms
by hand, waveforms embody the unbounded.

Sloth

Snug in crowns of cumaru & jatobá thick
with interlocking lianas, hung upside down
in meditation, a hairy yogi stilled ever stiller,

else rasta muppet whose fur teems with green
algae, scarcely movable feast replete with ticks
and beetles, nutrients that seep back through

a sedentary planet's skin, camouflaging it
from erratic orbits of harpy eagles & ocelots
but not preachers who see in ruminant stomachs

sluggishness of mind which neglects to begin good.
Yet God is made of *tempo giusto*. Like knowing
when to climb three-toed down a tree to shit.

Peacock

Upon a corbelled stone wall, a thrall of eyes
peers from a train draped iridescent across
mid-afternoon, embroidered from Saturn's

rings perhaps, lustrous with crescent sheen,
burning bright blue & green like a dare
not to take seriously the premise of intelligent

design. How feathered audacity weighs
proportionally more than a bejeweled crown
upon a king's bald pate. What roving beak

knows it's festooned with a drum major's tom,
imperial & startling. When an ostentation
of birds constitutes an unarguable aesthetic.

for Mark Doty

Indian Elephant

Under date palms & a towering *gopuram*
studded with carvings of deities in acrobatic
sexual congress, it's almost easy to overlook

the dark, mustached mahout in khaki shorts
leaning against a crooked stick, murmuring
in Malayalam to the ornamented purveyor

of blessings beside him, bedecked in marigolds,
spirals of white paint outlining wistful eyes
and plummeting down a trunk that swings

to pluck a rupee from the devout, to bless
the bent-headed. In one practiced motion,
the prodigious converts into the propitious.

for Priya Sarukkai Chabria

Before Monsoon

Heat so oppressive that stray dogs
only lift their heads towards the butcher
shop where a cleaver thumps,
before settling back down under a goods

carrier or the shade of a thatched shack
which announces in large, arsenic
green block letters, "Lifetime cures
for piles or fistulas."

A rickshaw driver has wrapped his face
with a soaking *dhoti* & lies supine
in the back seat, refusing to take fares
while flies swarm thickly around a mound

of garbage a bearded ragpicker sorts
through with a blunt sapling,
preserving the odd item, preferably edible,
in a fibrous sack slung upon his back.

The golden rule here is inefficiency:
streets littered with half-begun houses
long-abandoned to a patina of red dust,
queues snaking in front of both clinic

and cinema, never seeming to advance,
men without protective headgear
hammering at a massive concrete flyover
while potholes gape in the crumbling road

a family of Jains bundled in white robes
crosses, their mouths covered to keep
out insects, their possessions balanced
upon their heads. How the sublime spills

into the scatological here with no apparent
contradiction, shrines popping up
from the grime of overpopulation
like toadstools after rainfall, a Ganesha

delicately carved in terracotta bobbing
on the dashboard of a truck that hauls
cow dung to villagers who use it for fuel,
a garland wallah doing brisk business

selling lotus flowers in an alleyway damp
with fresh urine. How the city points out
evidence of a seamless continuum:
heavens, earth, underworld—conjoint.

forRajni Shankar-Brown

Sounds

Depending on their shape, different rooms,
unoccupied, produce particular sounds
we lack a vocabulary for, gradations of silence

that turn ghostlier the higher the ceiling,
that deepen or disperse in echo the thicker
the surrounding foliage pressing against

whatever material the wall is made from,
whether fieldstone, brick, plaster, or wood.
To hear something without being able to name it

is a form of recovery & a source of frustration
which has at root an obsession with control
that can never be fulfilled, not in this lifetime.

Box Turtle

Jeweled egg in the middle of a twisting
path tamped down by footfall, darkened
in the shadow of tall pines, I pluck & put

it to my nose. Gradually, like arousal
rousing by degrees, a blunt head extends
from an uncircumcised prepuce to glare

red-eyed at how earth has been robbed
from under it, how it flails three-toed
in space. Until abruptly a hinged plastron

snaps shut. Gathering itself in, domed shell
concentrically radiating orange & black
in a mantra: hermetic, tantric, self-reliant.

Wild Turkeys

Not a murmuration of starlings or a watch
of nightingales, but a group all the same,
more like a comic troupe, puffed out

with reddish wattles, warty caruncles,
& seersucker wings that are rarely used
except to propel the bird in imitation

of flight that ends in flop. Toms & hens
have both poured out of an unseen clown
car, & they gobble, gab, cluck, cackle

their way through fields in search of grub,
spurred birds that are easy to laugh at,
easier to exalt. They are nothing like us.

Precipitation

Overhead, massed gases grow ever grayer,
blotting out shafts of light from reaching
the fern-gorged, trunk-spotted forest floor.

The rain, once it starts, wavers in rate
& pitch, moving from full pour, to mist
of droplets, to lightly cascading sheets,

never stopping entirely, turning branches
of the taller trees into makeshift canopies
which, once critical volume is surpassed,

will dump rainwater in a whoosh to turn
damp soil even boggier than before. Awash
in mush like coffee grounds. Soaked sounds.

Gator

To call it lethargic would be hyperbole,
because the lozenge of scales is like a log,
immobile in the mudflats even as I approach

with tentative steps to stand ten feet away.
No indication that the air shifts between us,
though I might just harbor malice, a half-

thought to fling a stone to see what rise
it gets. No sense of who's the predator,
who the prey, though the impulse to harm,

once formulated, takes hold like a pair
of jaws nearly impossible to pry back open.
Lurks still in the mind. Appetite incarnate.

String Solo

Is it a sound, thrush-gasp or throaty whimper, you
keep wrapped in wax paper for midwinter nights,
two hands & a vowel for company? Do longed for
fragments sing long enough to tilt wheel on axis,
spill? Slipped strap, tippled glade, lace in fretwork,
slow bloom of shoulder blade, clasps to unclasp,
lamplight on hairsheen, orchids blooming at the
wrists, gullies to swim in, the hour elongated,
shivery, a smell to carry off on the thumb, peaty
& overripe, but disappeared too soon, turned
muzzy. Jutting into the hour like craving for mar-
malade, how thickened past touch the pastiche?
An urgent, inclement burst of syrupy weather
that drenches the doer in doing, a mellifluous,
jagged syntax that when recalled will not be real,
not even close? Will any ecstatic dust remain like
cardamom between the fingers? *Camerado*, all I
know is the cello in imagination makes music
less sweet than hearing its body vibrate before us,
clenched between knees, flayed by a bow, cradled
at the base of the neck.

Cascades

Eddies hasten in rivulets of foam that over
time will gnaw into ground rock sure as drill
bits, but now froth like a bridal veil tossed

from ferry to flail against algae-encrusted
outcroppings with the sound of a thousand
whispers modulating in urgency—*over again*

& onwards—how wind shears the surface
of planks of light to leave burbling rumors
that water in motion defies its own finitude.

There beyond a crook, increased ad libitum
into tumult, terror, sheer boundlessness—
a horsetail's giant, discordant spray roars.

for Nancy Kuhl

Manatee

Past divided highway separating strip
mall from strip mall, a sinuous dirt road
ends at an overlook that unlike other

Floridians in the business of creating
& frustrating expectation has a half-
dozen nearly inchoate shapes floating

on cue, mottled portions broken from
primordial sludge, podgy ruminants
blotched brown, hardly discernable

from silt-choked water, backs encrusted,
two nostrils surfacing to snort breath,
before hunkering back into the deeper down.

Slate

Slagheaps of stone once an ancient sea
floor, now metamorphosed into foliated
slabs that jut in cragged angles breakable

along two planes of cleavage & grain
by splitters who lounge with lunch pails
and idle pit hammers beside a rusted-out

compressor, eyeing us warily. In a haze
of dust, we trace the mottled texture,
gray-green flat enough to hone a knife on,

durable enough to use for sill & lintel,
billiard-table bed & grave marker. Nouns
unlike our fingers: resistant to weathering.

Bulldozer

Bifurcated into multi shank rippers fitted
with tungsten steel alloy tips & a corrosion
resistant dozer blade with carbide strip

cutting edge, armed by six hydraulic arms
to level land, grade quarries, pile silage,
push snow, clear shrubs, erect earthen

barriers, dig moats, gouge burnt-out
vehicles from roadsides, construct field
fortifications, flatten homes to stone.

There, tree-stark under crisscrossing
power lines, twilight a gradually graying
voile, its big treads still. Utter as tableau.

for Ethan Paquin

Bumblebee

How a well-machined hairy orb bobs yellow-
breeched philosophy: foraging optimally,
visiting the vertical inflorescences of foxglove

from bottom up, pumping palp & maxilla
with the precision of pistons, no wasted motion,
searching under the sepals of monkshood

like a furtive lover, or like a German engineer
in the heliotrope, loading full corbiculas
with sticky pollen, moving bloom to bloom,

then back to a comb lodged between springs
of a truck cab seat rusting in green rushes.
Back to dance an alphabet of honey & wax.

Plumbing the Deepening Groove

That survival is impossible without repetition
of patterns is platitude – see moon rise or whorls
in wolf fur –

but how explain the human need to reenact
primal dramas,
even when the act perpetuates a cycle of abuse?

The boy who hides in the tool shed with buckle-
shaped welts
rising like figs from his arms will curse his father,

and in turn beat his son. Like a wave anguish
rises,
never understands itself before emptying in a fist.

The spurned daughter will seek out lovers who
abandon her,
self-will degenerating in the face of what feels
familiar.

Childhood, seen in light of recurrence, takes on
the heft
of conspiracy, casts a shadow across an entire life,

making it appear that nothing could have happened
differently, that free & easy is the stuff of semblance.

Then of the prerogatives, reclamation is principal,
to appraise the past the way a painter subsumes old
canvas

with new layers of paint, each brushstroke unconcerned,
sure, dismantling the contour of what once was realized

so that new forms can emerge to contradict the
suggestion
that survival is impossible without repetition.

Dust

Congregated in loops of dirt & hair
beneath the dresser, raining down
in shafts jabbed through vinyl slats

of shades that on closer inspection
are coated filmy enough to rub off
on the fingers, rolling from unpaved

roads in clouds, particles quivering
in the atmosphere to form nuclei
for condensing raindrops, gossamer

chaperone trailing tippet to comets,
absorbing & reddening starlight,
mote chanced to be born, like us.

for Ken Buhler

Willard Pond

Across the pine-fringed pond, a loon croons
once, twice, easily three times it fills the air
with half-laugh, half-warning. Beautiful & alien

to share the planet with such emanations,
to recognize in a sound no classically trained
tenor could exactly produce, kinship, a sense

that the distance between the alternate
universes human & bird inhabit is smaller
than ever imagined & more astonishing.

The loon pierces misty dawn a final time.
Once the urge to possess the sound passes,
I plunge, headfirst, into shimmering water.

Straw Barn

Bales beat sleek by rain lie like heaps
of corpses or a formula for calculating
some numerical quantity that will remain

uncounted, even when stacked in the barn.
Birthing damp odors that permeate deep
within its fibers, alkali blooms silica

fumes, a moist rot eating the closeted
air, seeping into clapboard panels,
into iron tines of the pitchfork hanging

its forged head behind hinged doors, flag
to a country that erodes season after season,
until its governance turns back to cows.

Tomato

Blazing evidence ideation too often trumps
concresence: for years shunned, uneaten,
red globe hanging death on serrated leaflets.

Wolf-peach. Love apple. Cutworm harbor
thought fleshy kin to nightshade until a colonel
ate a bushel in front of a courthouse & crowd

of over two thousand in Salem but did not die.
Sprawled in the square of my raised bed garden,
overhanging cages hairy stalked, riotous even

when unseen deer have nipped yellow tips
to nibs, finally after three near-rainless months,
one pendulous, ruddy fruit. Supple yet firm.

Yellow Blusher

Sodden with rainwater, the yellow-capped
mushroom has swollen, hangs over its thin stalk
so copiously, it appears the next drop of water

will prompt the entire venture to topple,
which is illusion, like the appearance of oneness
that's contradicted by a spongy underside,

network of papery layers, gills that hold up
the campanulate cap which comes off
as slime when rubbed by inquisitive fingertips.

This mottled, tenuous fungus, so easily snapped
from the soil, speaks in tongues the old growth
forest is not conversant in, except after rain.

Surface Tension

Scarified now but how? When we once heard
parades from windows, swayed in artificially

luminescent reeds under the Brooklyn Bridge,
filled soaked corn husks with masa dough,

glimpsed mouse-deer scamper on wish-thin
legs, called each other *mon petit coeur de sucre*,

split each other like oranges at the navel,
turning pith to string between wet fingers.

Our realm was the back of doors, ill-lit alleys,
laying splayed out on a lake dock baked in sun

until the impulse to jump. We were gods
caught in a rising soap bubble, arms bare,

upswept scent of sand dune barren as moon
except for us twinned, intertwined, tied

to nothing but in the moment each other.
Where did you go? Suds, not love, evaporates.

Double Rainbow

Speeding, without destination, after dark
torrents have poured & been returned
at home, the skies above mirror my mood,

windshield wipers knifing through sheets,
back roads slick with pooling, when a shard
of cloudlessness opens. Pulling over, cutting

the ignition, I unstitch myself from the humid
seat, still fuming, to greet a full spectrum
of color arcing past the treetops in lockstep

with its fainter inverse. Archer's bow, hem
of the sun god's coat, bridge between worlds,
reconciliation & pardon. They don't last.

Ants

One is never alone. Saltwater taffy colored
beach blanket spread on a dirt outcropping
pocked with movement. Pell-mell tunneling,

black specks the specter of beard hairs swarm,
disappear, emerge, twitch, reverse course
to forage along my shin, painting pathways

with invisible pheromones that others take
up in ceaseless streams. Ordered disarray,
wingless expansionists form a colony mind,

no sense of self outside the nest, expending
summer to prepare for winter, droning on
through midday heat. I watch, repose, alone.

Heron

Endued in shadow, still upon a complacent
pond-surface flecked with mid-afternoon,
stippled in the negative space of branches

branching, we nearly overlook your berth
on banks that emerge into the Blue Ridge
eventually. Quiescent, born into slower

time than flitting gaze, not yet croaking
quark-quark-quark to celebrate nightfall,
gradual as a coastal shelf, you readjust

a long neck, slim beak, settle in to stalk
the water. Inscrutable even before suddenly,
dart-quick, your neck unreels to stab a fish.

for Gregory Bruen

Mink

Skittish-eyed, fleet of paw, dens in a drift
pile or stream bank, stealthy, circumspect,
prowling the dark shore on paws alone,

hunting muskrat, crayfish, frog, skulking
miles at a time in night's percussion
section, pelt glistening even after the moon

slides from sight, more lustrous submerged,
a bolt of brown darkening under the water,
a crepuscular muscle uncoiling, emerging

to forage in forests led by a leash of scent.
Solitary codger, lithe, furbearing, thorough,
wanted for earmuffs & by horned owls.

Mohegan Sun

Where Uncas once wore a wampum collar
hand-carved from purple quahog clamshells,
a mammoth anodized rose looms, reflective

& stainless off the interstate. *Come play!*
a bunting stretched over the road trumpets
and to descend the climate-controlled

elevators into the clockless gaming floor
pulsing with color is to uncover a spectacle
broadcast on a wall of monitors: the fourth

circle of Hell, where avarice & excess
roll boulders back & forth, from Slotopoly
to the baccarat table. Time & again, I lose.

for Jerry Williams

Bullfrog

An act of theft, I admit, that compelled me
to pile asters & gladiolas in the car, surfeit
from a dark shed hid on the fringe of Harkness

Mansion where an upmarket wedding of two
bankers had taken place & I poured drinks.
A full two days later, after flowers had been

planted, jiggers soaked, I reach into the back
seat for a book & discover a twitching dirt-
clod which feels clammy, mucus-moist enough

in my fist that I recoil, unable to grasp hold
of elongated anklebones or breathing skin.
Instead I need to use a rag to scoop & fling.

Mosquito

Though I've shut my windows, scotch taped
any holes, doused myself in Deet, and flap
my arms with the avidity of a baton twirler,

you're there, nipping at my skin, hanging
like a sun spot in the periphery of my vision,
blood-hungry, persistent, an incarnation

of appetite that appears from nowhere,
impossible to drive away until indignant
mounds of flesh have already risen to mark

passage, by which point, infuriating speck,
you've vanished in epiphany: in the act
of feeding on me, you discover what you are.

Deer

Is foliage really tastier by the roadside?
Wonder weighted with sarcasm. A white-
tail deer grazes inches from my right

fender, apparently oblivious to the fact
that I've idled the engine to stare at him,
his bicycle-seat head hunched to munch

some ferns, to disdain others, all the while
edging around my car as if it were a natural
extension of the forest from where he's come.

Suddenly, mid-chew, a dart of panic lodges
that he springs up, jackrabbit-ears quivering,
to bound away on impossibly skinny limbs.

Skunk

Rolling right turn onto Signal Hill Alley,
clouds suffused with intimation of dawn,
dim, massive parking garages up ahead.

Just past where asphalt's striped white
for crosswalk, a hump of fur the selfsame
color, past scurrying. A foot away, I open

the car door to lean into battery innards
doused with Old Spice then lit with a match.
Mephitis mephitis. Double foul odor.

Bead-eyed, forepaws extended, scrunched
in repose, bisected by the median, deserted
with me before sunrise. Our minds' not right.

after Robert Lowell

Dragonfly

Darting blue shard the length of a toothpick
with enough nerve & agility to mate in midair,
to snatch midges from a hovering swarm

faster than the purple martins will snatch it,
each blip in its fractal flight an insect eaten.
Compound eyes made from thousands of eyes,

motion in all direction, pale soft naiad bodies
hardened with exoskeleton, grown into wings
that shimmer afternoon with rapid translucence,

turning the planked boardwalk along the lake
into a darning needle's sketch of cross-stitches.
In time, they'll sew shut your eyelids & lips.

for Lisa Russ Spaar

South of Hebron

Across the onion fields, a hulk of rusted metal groans,

as out of place, it seems to the boy whose father tills

the land, as an orange blossom unfurling in a smokestack,

but there it is regardless, its turret swiveling like a broken

carousel, leaving a streak of flattened stalks in its wake.

The boy lives here. Picks his way probingly around traces

of mines to hear his language spoken in collapsible stalls

of the village market's measly remains. He has nothing

to hurl in his house, has to scour bulldozed quarries

for fist-sized rocks that slice heavily through the air,

meeting stray man or metal with satisfying thwack.

How small the rock is compared to the singular burden

of being made unwanted in a land you were born in,

for perpetuity, for no reason you will ever understand.

for Mahmoud Darwish

The Well

Granite-willed, a wall encloses the well
where a rusty bucket teeters on a hook,
its bottom blooming with algae patches.

Years since anyone lowered the bucket
or there was drinkable water, yet as mute
testament to another time, a marker

of those who once tread the field among
cattle & square bales of hay, no shrine
would better suffice than this old tool

burrowed through topsoil, loam & sand
to tap an underground stream: whatever
we were & are now, such water knows.

Armadillo

Encrusted in granulated bands, parabolic
but for a tail tapered to an awl, methodical,
hairy-bellied, lizard-clawed, descended,

according to wheezy diner folklore,
from fugitives broken out of a traveling
circus that toured Smyrna in the thirties

with flatcars full of animal curiosities
& cirqueros, like the Human Volcano,
or achondroplastic dwarves who juggled

on top of hippos. Only the nine-banded
armadillos escaped. Still scour parched
earth for ants. No answer but in themselves.

for Terri Witek

Snowfall

Particulate as ash, new year's first snow falls
upon peaked roofs, car hoods, undulant hills,
in imitation of motion that moves the way

static cascades down screens when the cable
zaps out, persistent & granular with a flicker
of legibility that dissipates before it can be

interpolated into any succession of imagery.
One hour stretches sixty minutes into a field
of white flurry: hexagonal lattices of water

molecules that accumulate in drifts too soon
strewn with sand, hewn into browning
mounds by plow blade, left to turn to slush.

Vermont Casting

Shriveled leaves were a mistake, retained
enough damp to smolder the lighter's spark
into smoke that seeps from cast iron edges

in defiance of flue's creosote breath into lungs
of gray sky mottled overhead like thermal
underwear stretched too far past its elastic

band to snap back. Another summer slimmer,
I poke in charred stems, an anatomist of ash,
wondering how to stack the wood to catch.

Heraclitus would have the origin of all things
everliving fire in which souls come into being
& pass away. It's the burning, not what burns.

Compost

Filling a tarp full of spindled elm leaves
that cling & loosen in wake of dragging,
I stumble over frost-bitten lawn yawing

behind the yard into unbounded county
land where once dark falls ember-eyed
raccoon emerge to stride to the very lip

of the forest green high-impact garbage can,
where minutes molder the shape of cored
fruit, print ads, slightly fetid plastic bags—

all torn loose & strewn this winter night
I cannot sleep. Where I thought I was safest,
alone with stars & a rake, I'm startled.

for Gabrielle Calvocoressi

Dark

Ten minutes ago, there was gray in the sky,
now there's none, not a splotch of contour
& when I walk, I listen for gravel to crunch

underfoot so I don't end tooth in bushes.
Darkness in New England has a flavor close
to anise, a texture plush as peat moss, fills

the ear with cricket chirps, creaks with trees
amending their branches, smells like inside
a new shoe when there's still tissue paper

crumpled in the toe, feeds full on paranoia,
bloats the walker with blind urge to run
summarily offset by the necessity to grope.

for Rand Richards Cooper

Fireworks

Above the crenellated fringe, trees in full leaf,
a ribbon of light shrieks to unravel a pinwheel
that hangs in rumble, then dissipates sulfuric

and immediate, only to be replaced in the dark
by staccato bursts that flare incandescent citrus
shapes glowing bright & brief until outlines

recede in afterimage washed by the wake
of a maroon from whose report grow sudden
chrysanthemums unfurling saltpeter blue petals

trailing attenuating willows, sprays of spark,
black powder waterfalls reprised in smokescapes
that strobe & buzz of pseudo-stars: evanescence.

Blood

Marrow-sprung, eucharistic fount, black
pudding beaten in a bucket, kept
from coagulating, final taboo sopped

in a tampon or gargling from a slit
carotid artery, left to darken in air
like sunset stored in citrated vials

for transfusion, thimblefuls of grape
juice, wedding ring on a leach finger,
brackish foodstuff for the undead,

not wrung from turnips, no denser
than porter, it flows filtered forward,
pumps from valves until it clumps.

for Vivek Narayanan

Small Town Catechism

His cedar barn reeks of anise & gasoline,
a riot of tires loosely circumscribing its perimeter,
any vision of metropolis two thruways & a train
away or nodding through static on the tube.
However he hopes to pare himself, it's enough

to remain a fixture, like a garden implement
in the grass, turning surely into a truer self of rust.
His wife pots herbs into soil, but won't suck
him off the way he likes, even when a stone
wall lies between them & the nearest neighbor.

When he tells the story of his life to himself,
it's not cinematic, but withheld in abeyance
to some curve of space that claims his home
an unforgotten fleck in distant spokes of stars.
If things are how he says they are, who knows?

for David Cappella

Bats

Gathered in trestle-dark, colonial while day
burns, clawed toes curled, chiroptera turned
inward, the tires & feet crossing Congress

remiss to its sleep until dusk begins to verge,
the initiated to emerge in clumps that amass
on the hillside & upon the bridge. Hanging

around until one, then three, then trickles
that turn to runnels fill an exiguous band
of early evening with uncountable numbers—

divergent, highly patterned flight diffusing
in the far sky, carrying away pieces of us,
a maelstrom too faint to see, turning to ellipsis…

for Robin Beth Schaer

Fireflies

Heavy-draped beyond the slipform stone
wall laid one over two, two over one
& shimmed by thin fingers of granite,

night falls moonless in a bindweed field
stretching to a dark grove that flares light—
sudden, incessant, nitric – electric sea-green

bursts more frequently seen on an arcade
screen, signals a synchronous Morse code
of mating sent from lanterns rung in a rosette,

innervated by neurons, souls of the dead
in Japanese folkore, hotaru. Actually, it's love:
They only find each other in the dark.

for Niloufar Talebi

Lake with Human Love

Seen from canoe stem on a moonless night
the cosmos stretches boundlessly above,
a panoply of stars & the whitish curve
of the Milky Way, leaving the lone paddler

significantly insignificant, utterly diminutive
yet part of some larger, grander tapestry
unable to fully fathom. Human love is like
that, for when it appears, it affirms the person

before us, not as a projection or a romantic
ideal, but as who our beloved in actuality is.
When you love, it is paradoxically not you
who love but love which acts through you,

imbuing the mortal life with divine purpose.
The stars & the lake are one with the craft
moving through the water & the letter J
being inscribed in an eddy only to dissolve

& be written over again & again is one
with the breath of a body stilled into motion,
& the midnight excursion & landscape
it takes place in are metaphors for the union

of two souls who are companions & lovers
& friends. There's the real physical work
it takes to move forward, the synchronicity
in the curve of moon, intermittent headwind

rippling shadows & startling loon-cries,
all flowing both outwards & inwards
at once, not manmade nor projected from
the ego, but really there & revealed to us

in small daily acts of relatedness that help
texture the mysterious fabric of our lives.
Then there's the solitary figure in the canoe,
alone because one must be self-sufficient

before becoming successfully part of a pair,
yet not alone because the motion conspires
to claim otherwise. Say somewhere around
the bend the beloved waits, not to be loved

but to love, not to fulfill desire but to move
beyond it, not to possess but to share with
like the living pact between space & time,
water & craft, that brings us together as one.

For Michael Weisberg and Sharon Pacuk

ACKNOWLEDGMENTS

The author would like to thank his friends and family around the world and particularly the many poets who helped him shape this collection. He would also like to thank the editors of the following publications in which poems from this collection appeared:

Academy of American Poets: "Crossings"
Almost Island: "Blood" and "Sloth"
Ambit: "Sand" and "Willard Pond"
Barrow Street: "Primitives"
Blackbird: "Buzzards"
Bryant Literary Review: "Compost"
Big City Lit: "Stingray" and "Bullfrog"
Caduceus: "Deer"
The Connecticut Review: "Armadillo," "Bumblebee," "Manatee," "Mink," "Straw Barn," and "Sounds"
Divide: "Small Town Catechism"
Evensong: Contemporary Poems of Spirituality: "Peacock"
Fourth River: "Tideline" and "Yellow Blusher"
Fulcrum: "Plumbing the Deepening Groove"
Kaleidowhirl: "Fireworks"
Long River Run: "Heron "
Madison Review: "Before Monsoon"
Mascara: "Indian Elephant"
The Mississippi Review: "South of Hebron"
The New Hampshire Review: "Dark"
No Tell Motel: "Gator" and "Precipitation"
Noon: "Slate"
Open Letters Monthly: "Vermont Casting"
Redivider: "Box Turtle"
Second Avenue: "The Well"
Sentence: "String Solo"
Slope: "Bulldozer" and "Cascades"
Spinning Jenny: "Bats"
Tiferet: "Lake with Human Love"
Western Humanities Review: "Fireflies," "Palm Tree," and "Oyster"
The Wolf: "Mohegan Sun"

Thirty post-pastorals appeared in the chapbook *Seamless Matter,* the inaugural publication by Ohm Editions, an imprint of Rain Taxi Books.

Also from The National Poetry Review Press:

Lucktown by Bryan Penberthy

Bill's Formal Complaint by Dan Kaplan

Gilgamesh at the Bellagio by Karl Elder

Legend of the Recent Past by James Haug

Urchin to Follow by Dorine Jennette

The Kissing Party by Sarah E. Barber

The City from Nome by James Grinwis

Forthcoming:

Fort Gorgeous by Angela Vogel

Loud Dreaming in a Quiet Room by Betsy Wheeler

Please visit our website for more information:

www.nationalpoetryreview.com

CPSIA information can be obtained at www.ICGtesting.com
Printed in the USA
BVOW08s1331290913

332351BV00001B/2/P